GREATNESS INSIDE

*Seven Power Steps To Release The
Greatness Inside Of You*

Rebecca Simmons

Diligence Publishing Company
Bloomfield, New Jersey

GREATNESS INSIDE: SEVEN POWER STEPS TO RELEASE THE GREATNESS INSIDE OF YOU

To contact Rebecca Simmons to preach or speak at your church, organization, seminar or conference email:

rebeccasimmonsempowers@gmail.com

Connect with the author to join her network, the victorious woman academy, or for mentoring:

www.womendestinedforvictory.com

ISBN: 979-8-9869173-1-3

Printed in the United States

TABLE OF CONTENTS

DEDICATION

This book is dedicated to you and all of the powerful women and men who will read it and realize that there truly is greatness inside that has not yet been revealed for the world to see. You are sparkling on the outside, but there is greater on the inside, ready to burst forth and shine bright like a diamond.

Read this book and get it down in your spirit that the world needs what's inside of you. Make up your mind that there will be no more playing small – no more holding back – no more self-doubt!

Step forward and let your greatness shine and light up the world around you.

I dedicate this book to you, because although what I see on the outside is good, there's more. There is greatness inside.

TAKE THESE 7 POWER STEPS TO BEING YOUR BEST YOU, FINDING YOUR PURPOSE, AND ACHIEVING HIGHER LEVELS OF SUCCESS!

POWER STEP ONE

BE YOUR BEST

*Be not conformed to the things of this world, but
be transformed by the renewing of your mind.*
Romans 12:2

There's greatness inside of you! Yes you! There
is greatness in you just kicking and wanting
to get out; or maybe it's lying dormant for one
reason or another. Maybe someone put out your
fire by telling you what you couldn't do, shouldn't
do, or what they wouldn't do if they were you.
Maybe life happened, and you lost your dream of
one day being and doing something big, or at
least, something other than what you are doing
right now. Maybe there is a yearning inside of you
for something more.

Whatever the case, and wherever you find
yourself in life right now, I am so glad you are
reading this book, because I wrote this book for

you! I wrote this book to let you know that no matter how little or how much you have already accomplished, God is not finished with you yet. There's more. There's greatness inside of you that is yet untapped. It's time to release it. It's time to release the greatness that is still on the inside of you waiting to get out.

In order to release your inner greatness in full capacity, it is important for you to work on being the very best version of yourself.

Renewing Your Mind

As we grow up in this world from childhood to adulthood, we take on a lot of beliefs, attitudes, and behaviors that are not conducive to our being joy-filled, successful, and prosperous people. In order to have higher levels of success, we have to reverse the effects of our life experiences. We have to change the way we think about things and the way we act. Einstein is credited with saying, *"Insanity is doing the same things over and over and expecting different results."* Paul tells us in the scriptures in Romans 12:2 not to be conformed to the things of this world, but to be transformed by the renewing of our minds.

Renewing your mind allows you to gain practical insight into living your best life. It is necessary to erase old limiting mindsets, beliefs, habits, and destructive behaviors that stop you from being your best. This is done by replacing old thoughts and behaviors with positive, faith-filled beliefs and behaviors that benefit you and help you to get the results you want in life.

You must discard old mindsets, habits, and behaviors that do not line up with the plans that God has for you to live a blessed, prosperous and successful life.

I've learned from experience that in order to have the success you want, renewing of your mind, educating yourself in the areas where you are called to release your greatness, and personal transformation should be worked on every day. Don't overlook going back to school or taking classes to sharpen your skills or even to learn a new skill. Constantly look for new ways to grow in your area of expertise and influence. Take time to diligently read materials like the Bible and other books that will empower, educate, inform, and motivate you. When it comes to the Bible, keep in mind that you are not reading the scriptures to be religious or just to be able to quote the Bible. Joshua 1:8 tells us to meditate on and study the scriptures so we can make our way prosperous and have good success!

I view my Bible as a line of communication from God to me and as a blueprint that I use to conduct my life. I guess you can say, it's my spiritual GPS – God's Positioning System which orders my steps and gives me direction and faith to fulfill my purpose and live my dreams. The Bible helps me to have hope and to keep going when life hits me hard and I feel like quitting. It's also my way of nurturing my relationship with God, feeling His presence, and hearing His great plan for my life. Finally, the scriptures give me a great sense of identity and power!

There was a time when I felt pretty powerless in my life. Growing up, circumstances had really gotten me down. There were emotional chains holding me in bondage and barriers blocking me that I just could not seem to get through. I had been through sexual abuse, abandonment, rejection, failure, teen-age pregnancy, welfare, looking for love in all the wrong places, bad relationships, a failed marriage, and being broke, busted, and disgusted. I had landed at a place called "hopeless and just going through the motions." I had also picked up some pretty bad habits hoping to just feel better by way of self-medication. I was partying and drinking almost every night, and I was going from one bad relationship to another. Then one night, I met Anthony, my husband now of almost 27 years, in a bar in Newark. He invited me to church. At first I resisted going, but I finally went, and ended up joining the church. That was in 1994. My life has radically changed from that point forward! I no longer feel hopeless, angry, victimized, dirty, nasty, rejected, abandoned, or like I don't have value. I forgave the people who hurt me. I forgave myself. I received my true identity as a daughter of God. I changed my mindset, I gave up most of those bad habits (I'm still working on the junk food), I tapped into my purpose and power, and I live each day filled with hope for the day and for the great future that lies ahead for me. Even in hard times, I find myself with an inner joy and peace that surpasses all understanding. I am a woman on a mission, and I am manifesting victory in every area of my life! That's my story and I'm sticking to it!

God wants you to know your true identity and power. He wants you to be free from any chains holding you in bondage or any barriers blocking your path. John 8:32 says, "You shall know the truth and the truth shall make you free!" That includes being set free from any hindrances and barriers that stand in the way of you having all that God has planned for you to have in this life. The Bible is a powerful tool for success and victory. God speaks to us through the scriptures. Reading the Bible is our way of nurturing our relationship with God and hearing His great plan for our lives.

Work on personal development daily to transform your life, take control of your thoughts, behaviors, and emotions, and walk in your power.

The Shaping and Transformation of Your Mind
Our mindsets were, for the most part, shaped by our environment as we grew up. Most of us have some flaws in our thinking and we may even find our mind taking us places we really don't want to go. Even now, as an adult, if you don't guard your mind from the influence of the world around you, your mind will be bombarded with negative thoughts all day every day. If you allow the world to control your thoughts, you will find yourself fighting to find hope and positivity in this life. If the world forms your thoughts, your life will begin

to take shape according to how you think. Proverbs 23:7 says, "As a man thinketh, so is he."

What You Put In Is What You Get Out

A negative mindset will lead to a life filled with negative people, places, things, and actions. Your thoughts, inevitably, will begin to form your character, your actions, and your identity. That's why it's important to guard your mind and to feed your mind with positive and empowering content. In order to climb over the barrier of negativity, we must be transformed by the renewing of our minds. Total transformation can be manifested through the Word of God. Through the Scriptures, God has given us a biblical blueprint for success and prosperity. He has given us a transformational personal development program that will allow us to replace our old ways of thinking and doing things with His way of thinking and doing things.

Transformation Involves Change

It's time to change behaviors that are destructive to yourself and others. This includes smoking, getting drunk, using drugs, careless sex outside of marriage, cursing people out, having an unhealthy diet, and any other mistreatment of others or misuse of your body. Remember, your body is the temple of God. We must honor God in our bodies. Paul said, "When I was a child, I thought like a child, I acted like a child, but when I became a man, I put childish things away" (1 Corinthians 13:11). To be your best, you must change. Change is not easy but change for the better is necessary.

The following benefits are attached to focusing on transformational personal development every day:

Benefit #1: You become an overall better person.

When I suggest that you become a better person, I am not saying you are not a good person or that you are not good enough. I am saying that you have not reached the fullness of the potential that is inside of you to be your very best self. Many people are stuck in the status quo because they never take the time to reflect on who they are, what they have achieved so far, what they aspire to achieve, and what skills and knowledge they need to have in order to achieve what they aspire to achieve. More importantly, they never stop to think about and find out what self-limiting behaviors or characteristics are keeping them from achieving the success, happiness, or prosperity that they are seeking after.

On the other hand, sometimes it's not that they don't reflect on these things, but they are ignorant of the fact that they have issues that need to be resolved and characteristics or behaviors that need to be changed. People in this category are stuck and are sometimes not even looking for ways to get unstuck. There is a saying that what you don't know won't hurt you. I beg to differ. I say that ignorance is not bliss. One of my favorite scriptures says that people perish for lack of knowledge (Hosea 4:6). The Bible also tells us in Proverbs 4:5 to get wisdom and to get understanding. Getting wisdom is not just about getting head knowledge. It's not about just knowing what to do. Getting wisdom is about also getting a full understanding of the purpose and plan for your life, getting an understanding of where you fall short or where you can be better and then moving in the direction of making the necessary adjustments to your character and/or behavior so that you can be successful.

Benefit #2: You do not have time to focus on what other people are doing.

When you are working on yourself, it takes your focus away from what other people are doing. You become mission minded, with your ultimate mission being developing the greatness in you! You develop a laser-beam focus where you can't be distracted by what your neighbor is doing and whether they are having greater levels of success than you are having. You won't worry about the grass being greener on the other side because you will be fertilizing and watering the grass of your own life and purpose. When you have this kind of focus you don't covet, compare, or compete. You are in a zone knowing that what God has for you is for you and nobody can change that or take it away from you. I have this new saying, I'm a woman on a mission manifesting victory in every area of my life every day!" You must adapt a winning, unstoppable, focused mindset. You don't have time to focus on what other people are doing. That is a distraction. Stay concerned only about being your best so that you can get the best results out of the effort you put into what you are called to do.

Benefit #3: You are more content with yourself knowing that you are getting better every day.

There's something gratifying about setting goals to be and do better and meeting those goals! There is a great sense of accomplishment in knowing that you are better today than you were yesterday and that you are getting better every day. Keep setting your SMART goals. Stay on track to meet those goals (SMART Goals are goals that are: Specific, Measurable, Attainable, Relevant, and Timely). Celebrate your small wins. Keep a success file or journal. Take plenty of pictures along the way. Each time you finish a goal like writing a chapter of your book, or losing a pound or two, take some time to reflect on that victory and feel the feeling of satisfaction that you get from your successes along the way to total victory in obtaining that particular goal. One of the mistakes that I've made often is not taking time to enjoy the journey – not taking time to celebrate along the way. One day after I was getting ready to receive my Honorary Doctorate degree that I received on December 18, 2022, I heard God say to me, "Exhale. Breathe. You can enjoy this!" And I did! So take time to celebrate along the way. Enjoy the journey. Celebrate your small wins. You will have earned it!

Benefit #4: You have more peace.

When I changed my life for the better and started working on being my best self, I noticed that first of all, I had become a better person! Then, I also noticed that I had less drama going on around me. The more I changed, the less drama I was experiencing. Prior to changing my life and my mindset, it seemed like every day there was something new to bring me disappointment, stress, and despair. But with my new mindset and my new determination to live life in a different way with a Kingdom (royal) perspective, things just kept getting better. The drama went away, and I was able to live in peace for the most part. There were still occasions when things got out of hand or someone did something that would have normally stressed me out; but I was looking at life through a new set of lenses, and situations no longer had the power to take my peace.

The same will happen for you as you are transformed by the renewing of your mind. You will begin to think differently. You will begin to act differently. Things around you will change. People around you will change, and your response to the things and people around you will change...for the better. You will no longer be stressed out and ready to pull out your hair when things go wrong or when things don't go the way you want them to. Instead, you will respond with peace and confidence that everything is going to be all right. You will have an anchor in your soul that all things are working for your good. You will have peace in the middle of the storm. Why? Because God is the Master of the storm. It is your faith in God that will give you a peace that surpasses all understanding. As you become and walk in the authenticity of who God created you to be, everything in your life will align with His master plan for your life. Warfare will come, but your peace will come too as you remember and believe that no weapon formed against you can prosper.

And we know that all that happens to us is working for our good if we love God and are fitting into his plans. Romans 8:28

No weapon that is formed against you shall prosper; and every tongue that shall rise against you in judgment you shalt condemn. Isaiah 54:11

19

Benefit #5: You become more equipped for greater prosperity and higher levels of success.

Transformation is an inside job, and so is success! As you become a better you, you develop characteristics and skills that will lead to your success. When I study successful people, they all have one thing in common – they never stop working on themselves! They never stop learning. They never stop trying to find new ways to be better. They never stop practicing the skills they already have and working on skills that they may need to go to that next level. The more you develop yourself, the more you will grow as a person and the higher you will go in your quest for success in life. One of my favorite motivational speakers, the late Zig Ziglar often said, "Success is not what you achieve in the process. Success is who you become in the process."

Yes, there is a process when it comes to success, and the process will either make you better or make you worse. I say, better or worse, because some people lose their integrity on the way up and do not become better versions of themselves. Instead, they lose themselves while going after the mighty dollars and end up stepping on people as well as stooping real down dirty low just to make it to the top. But when you are transformed according to the Kingdom blueprint (the Bible), you become a better person. You become wiser. You gain a greater level of discernment. You know how to show yourself friendly, you know how to deal with difficult people. You grow in favor with God, and you grow in favor with man. Remember as you are developing into your 'best you' to ask God for wisdom. Solomon had an opportunity to ask God for anything he wanted. Instead of asking for riches, houses, or livestock, Solomon asked God for wisdom to lead the people. He asked God to equip him mentally so he would be able to lead the people! God gave him what he asked for, and He made him a very wealthy man as well. Solomon was noted to be the wisest man ever. He asked for help from God and, as a result, he was equipped to reign as king with wisdom and power.

Don't leave God out. Many people have a form of godliness, but no power and no impact. Do like Solomon did, and make sure you are praying in faith and making God a part of your life. Let God mold you and shape you into who He originally created you to be. Let Him fashion and form you for the assignment He created in advance for you to do. Let God equip you for your success and your prosperity. Your eyes have not yet seen, your ears have not heard, nor has it entered into your mind the totality of all that God has in store for you!

POWER STEP TWO

LEAVE THE PAST BEHIND

Brethren, I count not myself to have apprehended: but this one thing I do, forgetting those things which are behind, and reaching forth unto those things which are before, I press toward the mark for the prize of the high calling of God in Christ Jesus. Philippians 3:13-14

In the verse above Paul was saying, I haven't obtained that thing, but I press; leaving old things behind and pressing into the things that are ahead of me. One of the biggest traps that you can fall into is to dwell on negative things that have happened in the past. That's why the scripture tells us to forgive when someone offends us (Colossians 3:13).

Offense often brings physical or emotional pain. If someone stomps on your foot or punches you real hard, it brings physical pain. If someone violates you, betrays you, lies to you, or verbally attacks you, it brings emotional pain. Once you experience that physical or emotional pain, your next reaction is to get angry. It's almost like a reflex action that is built into us as people. You hurt me, and I get angry!

People often talk about the angry Black woman. It's somewhat of a stereo type because all Black women are not angry. However, I am certain that all Black women have been hurt to the point of that hurt making them angry at some time or another. I have a little testimony here. I was one who could be labeled an angry Black woman. I was molested when I was a child, my father was not in my life for many years after I turned ten years old, I was lied to by my first love, cheated on by the next man I fell in love with, and betrayed by a cousin who he cheated on me with. Can I tell you that I had anger stacked on top of anger?

Why was my anger so intense? Because I never let any of it go. The funny, but not so funny, thing is nobody ever told me not to be angry. I don't know if anyone even knew I was angry. The closest thing that I can think about anyone knowing is my sister Janice, God bless her soul as she is no longer with us in the land of the living. I believe my sister Janice knew I was angry

24

because when I first met my husband, she said to him, "You like her? She's a mean Black woman!"

I'm laughing as I write this because she tried to warn him. He didn't listen and had to find out for himself. I truly was a mean Black woman...because I was hurt. I was not only hurt, but I was still hurting. I had not let go of the anger and I had not let go of the pain. I had not let go of the past, and the past was holding on to me and preventing me from being happy and truly loving or receiving real love. Then one day, I heard a sermon about forgiveness. I still didn't let the past go. Shortly after that, I was at a woman's retreat, and I heard other women testify that they had been molested. Then the speaker, the late Dr. Gwendolyn Goldsby-Grant, who was a therapist, said powerful breakthrough words to them and to anyone who had experienced what they had experienced. The breakthrough words that she spoke that night were, "It's not your fault, and if you want to be healed, you have to forgive."

That was the day of my breakthrough! I received the fact that what had happened to me wasn't my fault, and I forgave the person who had done it. I then went on down the list and forgave everybody else who had hurt me. I forgave, and the anger dropped off of me. I let go of the past and the past let go of me!

You must let go of the anger, shame, and guilt of the past and be healed from the emotional pain that triggers bad behaviors or attitudes.

Sometimes we harbor ill feelings towards or even hatred of another person because they hurt us, but we have to let it go because as long as we hold on to the anger, the pain continues. Even though it may seem like you're not being hurt by harboring these feelings towards that person or people, you are. Bitterness, anger, and unforgiveness have a negative impact on your mind, your emotions, your health, your relationships and your life. You may have to go to therapy if the pain is too deep and you just can't stop feeling angry, bitter, hurt, or even depressed. Whether you go to therapy or not, try the next step and see how it works for you. The next step is forgiveness.

Are you holding anger and unforgiveness against someone? Let it go. Are you experiencing emotional pain because you were hurt by someone? Forgive them. Release them so you can be free. It was not your fault – whatever they did to hurt you. Receive that.

You must forgive people that have hurt you in the past.

Now I know this is not easy. Any time I talk about forgiveness, people tell me that they can't forgive or that I don't know what that person did to them, and the person or people that hurt them don't deserve to be forgiven. If that's your argument against forgiving, I say, you can forgive if you choose to and if you ask God to help you. I would also say that you're right. I don't know what they did, and they probably don't deserve to be forgiven, but you deserve to be free from the anger and emotional pain caused by that anger. Also, we have been commanded by God to forgive, so you must forgive. This will set you free from bitterness and anger.

Now it's time to forgive the person or the people who have hurt or offended you. How? Say, "I forgive so and so (whatever their name is) for what they did to me."

Do that for everyone you need to forgive. You might cry during this time of letting go, but those tears are washing away the residue of the pain that was locked up inside of you. From now on, every time you get offended and angry at someone, forgive them. Let it go! Forgive quickly. Don't nurse it. Don't rehearse it. Don't go running around telling everybody that will listen about it. Forgive it. Release it and keep it moving. Don't hold grudges. That will only keep you on lower levels of living. Grudges will lock you up and hinder you from living your best life. Forgiveness keeps you free so you can keep moving in power. That's right! Utilize this strategy to keep moving forward as you leave the past behind.

POWER STEP THREE

BE AUTHENTICALLY YOU

For we are his workmanship, created in Christ
Jesus unto good works, which God hath before
ordained that we should walk in them.
Ephesians 2:10

Know Your Identity

Who are you? Take some time to access who you are and what your likes, dislikes, goals, and aspirations are. So often, we get caught up in life, and we never really take the time to check in with ourselves to make sure we are in tune with who we are and the things we could be enjoying or doing in life. In the church world, it has gotten to the point where when you ask someone who they are, they will tell you, "I'm a woman of God." Or "I'm a man of God." or "I am a child of God." or "I am a child of the King." All of these statements are good, but they only give a definition of your positioning in God or in the Kingdom of God. The question becomes, "Who are you really?"

Others will answer in reference to their marital status, whether they are a parent or not, where they work or what their title or position is. We are getting close. I want you to take some time to reflect on the question of "Who are you?" and answer it. Take your positioning in the Kingdom, your status in life as a spouse or parent, your career or calling, and then add in your passions, your likes, and your favorite things to do. Add in your favorite actor, singer, speaker, song, movie, stage play, and/or Bible verse, quote, book or author. Even add in your favorite color, fruit, food, and beverage. Take some time to write it down. This is not for anyone's eyes but yours. It's an exercise to help you check in with yourself in order for you to get back in touch with that very special person – you.

Who Are You?:

_____

_____

_____

_____

_____

_____

_____

_____

_____

_____

_____

_____

_____

_____

_____

_____

_____

_____

_____

_____

_____

_____

Know Your Purpose

There is a divine purpose over your life. So many are walking around with no clue as to what they are supposed to do or why they are here. Do you ever find yourself wondering what your purpose is. Do you ever stop and ask yourself, "Why am I here?" Have you ever said to yourself, "I know there has to be more for me to do in this life?" or "What am I supposed to be doing next?" Have you ever felt yourself leaving one season of your life and not had a clue as to where God was taking you to next?

If you answered yes to any to any of these questions, you are not alone. I came to a point in my life in 2019 where I felt frustrated and stuck. I was doing a lot of work. I had the publishing company, I was helping other authors to publish their books, I was writing books, I was pastoring the church with my husband, I was preaching almost every other week and being called out to preach at churches and women's conferences. On top of all of that, I was a wife, a mother, and a grandmother. As you can see, I had plenty to do, but I felt like my season was shifting. I felt like I was supposed to be doing something else. I felt like I was supposed to be doing something more. But I could not find the answer as to what that something was. I prayed about it, but it seemed like the answer wasn't coming. Notice I said, "seemed like."

One day I went to a conference, and there was a speaker there from out of town. The moment the speaker started speaking, my belly began to quicken. My purpose and the greatness in me which had been lying dormant in my belly began to kick on the inside of me! After the service I went over to meet this person. Not long after that he became my mentor and shortly after that, he became my husband's mentor as well. My mentor was able to help me to tap into and identify my greater purpose and the greatness that was inside of me!

Finally, I was feeling alive again. I was beginning to see that although I was doing all of the other work, there was still more that I had to do. There was something that I was supposed to do to make a greater impact in the earth realm. The Bible says that God has already prepared good works in advance for us to do (Ephesians 2:10). I found the missing pieces to the puzzle of my purpose. That's why I birthed out *Women Destined For Victory*, where I empower ignite, and activate women to move past hindering obstacles, identify, embrace, and successfully walk out their purpose with power and release their inner greatness so they can have victory in every area of life as they make an impact in the earth realm.

I carried *Women Destined For Victory* around in my belly for over a year before I finally pushed it out. You may be feeling like you have no purpose, or you may be like I was and not really know what that missing piece of your purpose puzzle is. You're doing some things. You go to work every day. You may be a wife or a mother.

You may even already have your own business or ministry, but you still may be feeling like something is missing. That's your greater purpose lying dormant on the inside of you. That's the greatness kicking inside of you waiting to be birthed out. You just need to tap in and identify what it is. It's already in you. It just needs to be ignited and activated as you go into action living it out. You have purpose inside of you. You have greatness inside of you! It's built into your DNA. Your purpose was designed before you were yet in your mother's womb. It is tailor made for you. You can begin to identify your purpose by finding out what you are passionate about. Take this purpose activation assessment to help you to identify your purpose. Your purpose is wrapped up in the greatness that's inside of you.

Purpose Activation Assessment

1. What makes you feel alive? What are you passionate about?

_____

_____

_____

2. What breaks your heart or makes you angry?

_____

_____

_____

3. If there were no financial, educational, or experiential limitations, what would you be doing as an occupation or career?

_____

_____

_____

4. What are the occupations that are most prevalent in your family?

_____

_____

_____

5. What have you been named? What prophetic words have been spoken over you describing who you are or what you have been called to do?

_____

_____

_____

6. What do people come to you the most for (either for counsel, advice, or information on how to do something?)

_____

_____

_____

7. What do you find yourself doing a lot of on a regular basis (to make an impact, just for fun, or as a hobby?)

_____

_____

_____

8. What do you often dream about doing one day?

_____

_____

_____

9. What are some of the things that you love doing?

_____

_____

_____

10. What are you graced by God to do? In other words, what comes easily to you that you can do without much effort or practice?

_____

_____

_____

Look over your answers to the assessment questions. If you notice that you gave the same or a similar answer to two or more of the questions, you are close to identifying what you are here in this life to do. You are close to tapping into your inner greatness.

The next step is to pray and ask God to show you what your purpose is. Believe me, God will answer your prayer and reveal to you what your purpose is, or He will send someone into your life like He did with me to help you to identify your purpose. Just like my mentor and leader helped me, I help other women to find their purpose, and I hope I'm helping you in this book to find yours.

Once you tap into, identify, and walk in your purpose, you will be on the path to releasing the greatness that's inside of you and making an impact in the earth realm. Don't settle for just getting through life. Get through life on purpose. Live out your purpose.

Just a note here. As you identify your purpose, you may see others already doing what you were born to do. Don't let that stop you from doing what may appear to be the same thing or something similar. Guess what? They may be already doing it, but they are not doing it like you will do it. They may already have a large following, but there are some people who are assigned to follow you. There are some people that your voice and your purpose are assigned to. They need you to do your assignment in the earth realm. They need you to walk in your purpose. They are waiting for you! Don't compare yourself or compete with others. You have work to do. Keep your focus and walk in the purpose that God has already ordained for you.

Know Your Value

As I mentioned earlier, you are a very special person. You are God's creation. God's masterpiece. Get that down in your spirit and always remember that you are wonderfully and fearfully made, the top and not the bottom, blessed and highly favored by God, a Designer's original who has been birthed into the earth realm with greatness engineered on the inside of you. God created you with very specific works that He planned for you to do.

It's important for you to know and remember your value because life will knock you down, and people and situations will wage war against you to try to make you feel inferior, inadequate, scared, insignificant, and unworthy. When this happens, or even if it's already happened or happening, can I push you and encourage you to fight back? Fight back in knowing that the enemy of your greatness, or as we say in church, the devil is a liar, and the truth is not in him! You are precious in God's sight. When God made you, He broke the mold.

Walk In The Power of YOU

There is power in **YOU**. Walk in the power of YOU. YOU is my acronym for **Your Own Uniqueness.** There is no one on this earth like you, and no one can do the things that God has prepared in advance for you to do like you can. Hold your head up, square your shoulders, and walk in the power of your authenticity. Never compare yourself to others or feel like you have to compete with anyone to be seen or heard. What God has for you is for you. So dare to boldly be who God created you to be. Dare to be original. Dare to be authentic. Dare to be powerful. Dare to walk in your purpose with power and to be unapologetically, authentically, you.

Dare to be courageous and faith filled. Realize that what God has for you is for you and nobody can take it away from you. Dare to walk in boldness being who God created you to be. Be original. Be authentic. Be powerful. Walk in your purpose with power and be unapologetically, authentically, you.

POWER STEP FOUR

DON'T LET FEAR STOP YOU

For God has not given us a spirit of fear, but one of power, love, and a sound mind.
2 Timothy 1:7

As you walk in purpose, you have to look out for the number one purpose and success blocker – FEAR!

There is a widely used acronym for FEAR. The acronym is **F**alse **E**vidence **A**ppearing **R**eal. For a long time, I thought this meant that fear was not real. As long as I believed this, fear had power over me. Then I continued to reflect on the scripture, *God has not given us a spirit of fear, but one of power, love, and a sound mind.*

Let me break this down for you starting with the scripture. The Bible says, God has not given us a spirit of fear. So that tells us that fear is a spirit. It is a spirit that operates to stop you from moving forward in your purpose or in victory over whatever may be hindering your success. The way we deal with opposing spirits is to recognize that Jesus gave us power over every evil spirit that comes against us *(Luke 10:19)*. You have dominion over fear. That's why you can no longer allow fear to have dominion over you! You have already been given power and authority over fear.

Secondly, you have been given a Spirit of power (that's "Dunamis" in the Greek, which is dynamite power to supernaturally blow fear up into pieces and make it dissipate).

Thirdly, you have been given a Spirit of love, and the Bible tells us that perfect love casts out fear (1 John 4:18). Perfect love is the love of God. God's love is so perfect that He has set it up that no weapon formed against you shall prosper. The weapons will form, but you have power over them.

The fourth thing the Bible tells in this verse of scripture is that God has given us a sound mind. If I were preaching, I would shout out, "Come on somebody!"

You have a sound mind! What does that mean? It means when the spirit of fear comes to attack you, you have the ability to stop and think about what is really happening at that moment.

Why would fear show up at just that moment in time?

The answer is: To stop you! Fear comes to stop you – plain and simple!

Now let's go back to the acronym **F**alse **E**vidence **A**ppearing **R**eal. Again, I used to think this meant that fear was not real but fear always felt real to me, and the impact was real as well. I would freeze up or want to fight or run (these are all natural reactions to fear). My mouth would get dry, my legs would turn to Jell-O, and my heart would start beating a hundred miles a minute. I would get light-headed and feel like I was going to lose control of all of my bodily functions and maybe even fall out! Can you see how real fear was to me?

So, using the acronym with the understanding I had of it at the time didn't work. What did work was the scripture we just talked about and the new revelation that I received about fear. The acronym is correct. **FEAR is False Evidence Appearing Real.** The new revelation of that is this: False Evidence Appearing Real does not refer to fear not being real. We already came to the conclusion that fear is very real.

False Evidence Appearing Real refers to the **LIES** that **FEAR** tells you. The lie that you can't do that thing, or that people will laugh at you, or that nobody will like you, or nobody will support you, or you're going to mess up, or you're going to fail, fall short, fall out, get fired, lose, get hurt, or maybe even die! Lies! Lies! Lies! False Evidence Appearing Real comes to make you FEAR so that you won't step out in faith and even try! That's Fear!

We have to fight back when it comes to fear, because it can get to the point where we spend so much time living in fear that we get to the end of our lives and realize that we never really lived at all. Don't let that be your story.

The next time the spirit of fear comes to you, know that it didn't come from God. Know that you have power over it. Know that it won't prosper because God's perfect love set it up to fail. Know that with a sound mind, you are equipped to be intellectually aware of why fear has come.

Finally, refuse to believe the lies that FEAR whispers in your ear! Fill your mind and heart with the truth of God's Word which tells you that you can do all things through Christ who gives you strength! As far as the people and their response to or opinion of you, remember this: Who God has for you is for you, and who God has to be in your life, they will like you. They will approve of you. They will support you, and they will be cheering you on, pushing you to your position of success! They will have their hands in the middle of your back, pushing you to your destiny of victory. They will be pushing you to release the greatness that's inside of you!

"Don't be afraid of what people will think about you. remember this: Who God has for you is for you. You don't have to twist yourself into a pretzel to make people like you. Push past fear and being concerned about haters and naysayers and push to birth out your success!"

POWER STEP FIVE

HAVE GREAT RELATIONSHIPS

Do not be misled: "Bad company corrupts good character." 1 Corinthians 15:33

In order to have success in life, you have to make sure that you develop and nurture the right relationships. Have you ever heard of OQP? I created and started using this acronym in my teaching a few years ago. OQP stands for "only quality people." The Bible tells us that bad company corrupts good character. There's also a verse that says, be careful that you think you are standing unless you fall (1 Corinthians 10:12). Basically, what these verses are saying is watch the company you keep, because hanging out with the wrong people can take you in the wrong direction.

Prior to giving my life to God for Him to lead and direct me in the way that I should go, I used to do everything that I was big and bad enough to do. I drank heavily, did some other stuff, had quite a few bad romantic relationships, hung out almost every night and hung around people who were just as bad as or worse in these areas of their behavior than I was. As a result, I was digging a deep hole for myself that, had I continued in that direction, would have probably swallowed me up and killed me. I thank God that one day I was presented with an opportunity to make a U-turn, and I took it.

God allows U-turns. We just have to be smart enough to take the U-turn when we come to it. Maybe it's not even about being smart. Maybe it's about being sick and tired of being sick and tired. Like I was. I was sick and tired of being sick and tired. Are you smart enough or sick and tired enough to make a U-turn in that area of your life where you know you need to stop or change a certain behavior, habit, attitude, or result? If you are, God is speaking to you now and saying, do it now. Now is your opportunity to turn and make the changes that you need to make in your life. These changes will lead to your victory in that area where you have been stuck.

Now, look around you. Who are the people in your life right now that you relate to on a close or intimate basis? I'm asking about platonic friendships and relationships as well as romantic relationships. Are they adding to your success and greatness, or are they contributing to the habits that prohibit you from having success and embracing and releasing the greatness that's inside of you? Are they people who have conquered the bad habits that hinder them and found success in their own lives, or do they have the same bad habits that you do or that you are trying to stop? Do they have a winning mindset, or do they have a defeated mentality? Are they going to the top knowing and believing that the top is not too high, or are they settling for the status quo? Do they lead their lives in such a way that shows they have greatness on the inside of them, or are they on a fast path to a destructive crash?

If you had a lot of answers relating to the first part of each question, then you have a pretty good friend group. If your answers were mostly yes to the second part of each question, you probably need to reassess your friend group and begin to put some distance and time between you and them. I don't say this to be mean, but in some instances it's a matter of the blessed life or a messy life. Blessings or bad consequences. Success or failure. Which ones do you choose?

I remember when I was trying to quit some negative behaviors I had. I had a friend that I was very close to, and we used to hang out together and do some of the things I was trying to quit doing. I told her I was quitting doing these things. One day shortly after I told her this, I went to her house, and guess what? She had it all set up and laid out! The very things I did not want to do were right there in plain sight to tempt me. Right in my face. I left her place that night and never went back again. I made a decision that I wanted better. I wanted to win. I wanted better and to win more than I wanted this person as a close friend. I made a choice for better. I made a choice to win. She wasn't happy about it. She didn't understand the mindset that I was operating in. She took it personally. She thought I was getting new on her and accused me of changing. She probably thought I felt like, all of a sudden, I was better than her.

She was right in some of these areas. I was getting new, leaving the old behind. I was thinking different and acting differently. However, I didn't think I was better than her, I just knew that I was better than how I had been behaving when I was around her and even when I wasn't. This wasn't personal against her, but it was personal for me! From that point on, I chose my friends and associates according to where I was heading. I was heading to the top! I was heading to ultimate success! I was heading for greater! I told you this story to make the point that birds of a feather really do stick together. If you want better in your life, you have to hang out with other people who want better. If you want success, you have to hang out with other successful people or other people who want success.

Someone once said, if you have four broke friends, you're probably going to be number five!

Keep in mind that what I'm talking about here also applies to your romantic relationship. Make sure you are not allowing yourself to open up to a person who is all wrong for you. Sometimes you can give your heart to a person and that person turns out to be narcissistic, negative, toxic, abusive, or unfaithful. You really have to take the time to get to know a person before you let them into the secret and sacred places of your life. God tells us not to have sex outside of marriage for a reason. When you open yourself up to have sexual intimacy with a person, you are opening yourself up to having a soul tie develop with that person. Notice how in the early biblical days, all a man had to do was take the woman into the tent and make love to her in order to make her his wife. That's because there is something that God engineered inside of man and woman that when the two puzzle pieces of the male and female sexual organs come together, there is a locking in place that is hard to be broken.

Have you ever been in a relationship and had sex with someone and after the relationship ended, you had a hard time getting that person out of your system? Well, me too.

The reason it's so hard to get them out of your system is because a soul tie developed during the relationship through sexual or even emotional intimacy, and that soul tie is a hard one to break, but it can be broken through prayer. I'm not going to get into it too deeply here, but you must be careful while you are dating (hopefully on your way to marriage). I always say, don't even date a person that you will not consider marrying. Get to know the person on a friendship level first. Spend time talking and asking questions. Listen. I mean, really listen to them when they talk. If a person talks long enough and you listen, you will find out who they really are beneath the surface of what they are presenting to you or what they want you to see.

Don't give away your secrets, and don't give away too much information about how the last person hurt you or how every person you have dealt with in the past broke your heart. You are giving up TMI – too much information!

I always tell the ladies to leave a little mystery. Don't give all of yourself away so freely, let the man pursue you and put in the effort to find out who you are and those intimate details about you. The same for a man. Don't be too anxious. Don't be desperate to take the first woman that says she'll go out on a date with you. Both men and women, pray and let God guide you to the person you are supposed to spend the rest of your life with. Don't be thirsty or overly zealous when it comes to love. Don't run into his or her arms too fast, and do your best to stay out of those beds. Sex outside of marriage is like a pandora's box. Once it is opened up, it's hard to close it back. If it is opened to the wrong person, you open yourself up to being mistreated, cheated on, or even taken advantage of and made to look like a fool.

Ladies, guard yourself by only allowing yourself to be pursued by a quality man. Men, guard yourself by looking beyond the exterior and only pursuing a quality woman. Yes, she must be attractive to you, but make sure she has other good qualities besides her looks. Women, he may look good, but make sure he has other good qualities besides his looks. Most definitely, make sure that they are God-fearing, God-loving, individuals. I did not say churchgoing. You want to make sure that the person you are considering dating has a real relationship with God and that they live a life of integrity.

Overall, in order to succeed in marriage, relationships, business, or ministry, you need to have the right people around you. It's all connected. It's all intertwined. A wrong relationship in your life can block you from having success in one or more areas of your life.

Always Remember OQP.

Wrong relationships often lead to wrong behaviors and even wrong marriages which can stand in the way of your success in life. Right relationships lead to right behaviors and even right marriages which can propel you into higher levels of success and fulfillment of your God-ordained mandate or assignment in the earth realm.

POWER STEP SIX

EXERCISE DISCIPLINE FOR VICTORY AND SUCCESS

But the fruit of the Spirit is love, joy, peace, forbearance, kindness, goodness, faithfulness, gentleness, and self-control. Against such things there is no law. Galatians 5:22-23

So far in this book, I have given clear, practical steps for removing barriers, tapping into your purpose, and having success in your life. If you follow them, you will be systematically releasing the greatness that is inside of you for the world to see.

You see – there is more locked up in you than you even realize. You may be at the bottom of your ladder of success or very close to what you consider to be the top. However, you have not yet tapped into the fullness of the capacity of what is inside of you. There is greatness inside of you. There is another you inside of you. There are things that God has prepared in advance for you to do and you possess gifts, talents, skills, and abilities to do those things.

As you move forward in faith, obeying the calling of God in different areas of your life, God will begin to reveal more and more of what He has in store for you and what He has sent you here in the earth realm to do. As I mentioned earlier in this book, your eyes have not seen, nor have your ears heard, neither has it entered into your mind the things that God has prepared for you. Nor do you have a full realization of the things that God has put inside of you!

As you persevere and push, there is going to be a birthing, or a pushing out of destiny. As you continue to pursue God and His purpose for your life, there is going to be a great revealing of the greatness that's inside of you. '

We talked earlier about your purpose. Besides your purpose, there is a mantle and a mandate. The mantle is God's power or anointing on your ability to do the thing He calls you to do. The mandate is God's call for you to do that particular thing or more specifically, your assignment. Your mantle and mandate may be for the church, but contrary to popular belief, we are not all called to only preach or fulfill our mandate in the church. You may be called to the church, to government, to education, to entertainment, to technology, to family, to finance, or to another area in the mountains of influence in society. Pray and ask God to show you which one of the mountains of influence in society He wants you to occupy and then ask God to give you your mountain!

As you have done the purpose activation assessment earlier and began to have an idea of your true purpose, once God confirms your mandate or assignment, you will be able to go back and tie your purpose in with your mandate or assignment. You will not only know the reason for which you were born or for which you exist (purpose), you will also know what area you are anointed for and assigned to (mandate). This goes beyond purpose and into calling (another word for mandate). And remember calling is not always for the pulpit (although you ***do want*** to make sure you are also using your gifts to advance the ministry of the church that you are a member of).

Ephesians 2:10 says God created us with good works prepared in advance for us to do. Once you have identified what you are anointed for and assigned to do by God, you have to discipline yourself. Romans 12:2 tells us that we cannot be conformed to the things of this world, but we must be transformed by the renewing of our minds. That applies to all believers. We must change. We must change our behaviors to behaviors that are pleasing to God and conducive for our success in life. In order to do this, you must discipline yourself. What I have done in this book is what I call "stacking." I have stacked one principle on top of another into seven steps. The purpose is not for you to pick and choose the ones you like and put them into use. The purpose is for you to follow the blueprint and put them all into use so that you can, from faith to faith and glory to glory, release the greatness that's on the inside of you to the greatest magnitude. No more playing small, and no more settling for less than being and doing your best. Your refusal to play small and settle for less leads to you living your best life and receiving God's best.

After you read each step, put it into use in your life and keep it in use. Don't stop using one power step as you go on to grasp the concept of the next ones and put each one into action in your life. This is part of disciplining yourself for victory. Paul says, I discipline my body and bring it into subjection so that I do not become disqualified. (Paraphrased 1 Corinthians 9:27).

I've heard people use the excuse, "Well, the flesh wants what the flesh wants." That is true, but you have to discipline your flesh! You have to make your flesh line up with your intention and commitment for success and victory. You have to make your flesh obey you. You have power over your flesh!

Discipline yourself in what you think, say, do, watch, wear, eat, and drink. I'm not going to spend time telling you what you should or should not do in these areas. You pretty much already know that. I will tell you that you must discipline yourself so that the fullness of God's anointing can rest upon you as you pursue success in your mantle and mandate and in every area of your life.

Remember that bad company corrupts good morals, character, and behaviors. In order to be fully used by God, you have to let Him clean up your life. If you have some sin in your life, give it to God. Ask Him to help you to discipline yourself to let that thing or those things go. You cannot serve God and your fleshly desires and expect to be great. God will elevate you and your flesh will sometimes take you on a low path. There is a definite war between the flesh and the spirit. You will not be able to satisfy them both simultaneously. You will eventually have to let one go. Which one will you choose? Let me help you. Your blessing is with God who only has good things in store for you. He is the one who put the greatness on the inside of you, and to top it off, your body is His temple – His Greatness dwells in you. Your flesh, if allowed to be in control, will only lead you to destruction.

The Power of Saying No

There is power in saying no. There are some things that you will just have to say no to, whether it's bad behaviors or bad and negative attitudes that deter you from being the best version of yourself. Although I definitely have not totally arrived, I personally have been successful in disciplining myself in many areas of my life. One area that I'm praising God about is my temper. I used to allow people to get under my skin to the point of having my heart hurt. Do you know that the closer people are to you the more they can hurt you?

One person who has this ability in my life is my husband. There have been times when I got so angry at him that I would hurt like my heart

60

was really breaking in my chest. Then I got the revelation. In my spirit, I heard God say, "Daughter, that's the devil! He is just trying to use your temper and trigger you to get fuming mad, so you won't have any peace! Your husband is not your enemy! It's only the devil trying to get you caught up in your emotions. Don't let your emotions have that kind of control over you!"

Wow! That was a wake-up call for me! From that point on, I began to exercise discipline whenever my husband and I had an argument or a disagreement. I received another revelation. Here it is: "It's not that deep!"

The truth is, if we have a disagreement or argument, it's not the end of the world. Couples argue! Couples disagree! Just go to your respective corners, cool down, be quiet, think it over, and then come together and talk it out until it's resolved!

That's a solution for somebody working things out in your marriage. The Bible says, be slow to speak, slow to become angry, and quick to listen (James 1:19). Also, it says, don't let the sun go down on your anger (Ephesians 4:26). And how about the rest of that verse, "Be angry and do not sin in your anger?" What am I saying? In marriage and in other areas of life, discipline yourself to not only know the Word of God, but to do the Word. James says we should not be hearers only, but doers of the word (James 1:22).

Believe That You Can Succeed and You Will.

Okay, one last story on discipline and I'll end this chapter. In August of 2022, I was at my heaviest weight in years. I was obese and gaining weight day by day. I made a decision to join the gym. When my daughter and I went to sign up, they had us sit down with a trainer. She took a measurement of my overall body makeup and told me that I had 47% fat in my body. She went on to say, "You're half fat."

I laughed at that, and the trainer and my daughter laughed at me laughing. But it wasn't funny. I had eaten myself into a state of being unhealthy. I made up my mind then that I would no longer participate in yo-yo dieting. No more "lose weight quick," fad diets for me. I was going to discipline myself to lose the weight and glorify God in my body, and I had the faith that I could drop the weight and keep it off.

No matter what you are trying to achieve, as you go to higher levels of success and as you release the greatness that's inside of you, always remember that with God, you can do all things. Nothing shall be impossible for you!

With this in mind for my own life and faith in the power and greatness that is on the inside of me, I made a decision that I was going to be fit and healthy, I put together a program and stuck to it and seven months later as I write this book, I have dropped almost 25 pounds. The goal I set is to lose 50 pounds in a year. Slow, steady, and permanent is my plan. I discipline myself daily to stay on point.

Just like I have the victory over my temper and over my weight and my health, you too can discipline yourself. You can win if you have faith to win. You can succeed and release greatness in those areas of your life where you are struggling if you believe you can and utilize discipline in your life.

The struggle may be in your marriage or relationships, your family, your ministry, your business, your finances, your health or weight, finding and walking in your mandated purpose, being emotionally whole or physically healed, controlling your temper, or any other area, but whatever area it is, you can have victory in it! No weapon formed against you can prosper as long as you fight back. You have the ability to win. You have the ability to succeed in setting and meeting your goals. You have the ability to soar like an eagle as you release the greatness that's inside of you!

Always Do Your Best.

While you are working on the steps outlined in this book and even as you are disciplining yourself to win, there will be challenges, roadblocks, and setbacks. There will be times when you are low on energy and self-control, and there will even be times when you don't feel like doing what you know you need to do in order to win and have success. But hear me when I say this. You cannot play around with this. You have too much to lose. You must always do your best. Whatever you do, do it with all that is in you! Do not half-step.

When I was younger, I used to go out dancing, and they would play a song with the lyrics, "Ain't no half stepping!" When it comes to you walking in higher levels of success and greater prosperity, and when it comes to releasing the greatness that is inside of you, you cannot be out there half stepping. You have to give the thing you endeavor to do your best shot. Give it your best effort and commit to stick with it until you succeed.

I have a little great-nephew named Kayden. We call him Glam. When he was about four or five years old, I was visiting my Mom and sisters in Florida where he also lives. He's very competitive, and we would always race or arm wrestle. This day, I was arm wrestling him, and I let him win about three or four times. After I let him win for the third or fourth time, he looked at me with a deep examining look like he was trying to figure something out. Then he said to me, "Let's do it again. Don't let me win this time. Go all out! Go all out!"

Everybody in the room that was paying attention burst out laughing. "Go all out!" Boy! You are too smart!

So, guess what I did? I arm wrestled him again, and this time I won. Why? Because I went "all out." I went all out just like he told me to. Then he said, "Again. Again!"

He was so happy that I had given him a challenge and gone all out. The point here is when I went all out, I won. It's amazing the lessons we can learn coming out of the mouths of children. That's why I always remain in a posture of being teachable. When you remain teachable, you will always be in a position to receive increase. You will always be in a position to receive more and you will always be in a position to receive strategies to win. Whatever you do in this life, I want to encourage you to go all out! When you utilize the strategies given to you, and when you go all out and put your best effort into whatever you are endeavoring to do, you will win! You will have the victory! So, whatever you do, do your best! Go all out!

POWER STEP SEVEN

KEEP GOD FIRST

Jesus said unto him, Thou shalt love the Lord thy God with all thy heart, and with all thy soul, and with all thy mind. Matthew 22:37 KJV

As I come to the conclusion of this book, notice that I am writing this chapter last. In actuality, although it's listed as the last step, it's the first thing you want to put in place. You want to make sure that God is first in your life, and you want to keep God first every day of your life. In order for you to win and have success and victory, God has to be in it!

Remember we talked about purpose being the reason for which a person or thing was created? You were ultimately created for God's glory. God's glory is His praise, His radiance, His splendor, His shine! You were created to reflect God's glory in the earth realm. You were created for God to brag about you. You were created as a vessel to carry God's glory everywhere you go. That's right. You are a glory carrier!

Isaiah 6:1 and 3b says, *In the year that King Uzziah died, I saw the Lord, high and lifted up and the train of his robe filled the temple and ...the whole earth was filled with His glory.*

That was a prophetic vision given to the prophet Isaiah of God's plan for His glory to be revealed throughout all of the world. God's plan is for His sons and daughters to be the glory carriers to take His glory to the lost, the hurting, the hopeless, the homeless, the doubting, the unbelieving, the perishing, and the sick. God is using you and me to reveal Himself to a sometimes cruel and unbelieving world. In order for God to use you as His glory carrier, you have to have Him seated on the throne of your life.

Again, the Prophet Isaiah said, "In the year that King Uzziah died, I saw the Lord." King Uzziah's fault was that he influenced the people away from God instead of towards God. As long as Uzziah was on the throne, God could not be on the throne in the people's lives, so Uzziah had to go! Who is on the throne in your life? If Boo or Bae is on the throne, if your job or business is on the throne, if your ministry or the people you minister to are on the throne, if your husband or wife is on the throne, if your children or parents are on the throne, if food, alcohol, drugs, or sex are on the throne, God is not on the throne in your life. It's not that He cannot be, but God will not share His throne! God is jealous over you. He wants the best for you, and He wants to be number one in your life. I said He wants the best for you, and He knows that a lot of the things that would substitute for Him on the throne are not conducive for you having His best.

When God is not first in your life, it opens the door for the thief to come in and steal from you. The scripture says in John 10:10, "The thief comes to steal, to kill and to destroy, but Jesus said, I have come so that you may have life and have life more abundantly." He says in John 15 (paraphrased), Stay connected to me. I am the true vine. With me you will bear much fruit, but apart from me, you can do nothing!

A lot of people will argue that you can have success without God being first in your life. I would disagree with that. You can do a lot and accomplish a lot of things without God being first in your life, but your success will not be complete and real without God being first in your life. Why?

You may ask. The answer is because the door is still open when the throne is occupied by anything or anyone other than God. When the door is open, the thief can come in to steal your peace, your joy, your health, your marriage, your mind, your money, and whatever else there is to steal. Shut the door on the enemy who wants to keep you separated from God. Keep God first in your life and you will not only be a glory carrier, but you will see the blessings of the Lord manifest in your life. Remember Jesus said He came so that you may have life and life more abundantly. Life here in the Greek is Zoe. Zoe is the blessed, abundant, joy-filled life that comes from trusting in the promises, provision, and power of God.

Give God the Glory

As you keep God first and allow Him to order your steps, the blessings of God will be released in your life. As you meditate on the Word, day and night, delighting yourself in the Word of God that is contained in the Bible, you will make your way prosperous and have good success and everything you do will prosper. As you walk in obedience to God, you will be blessed when you come and when you go. As you pray and believe God, He will expand your territory, bless you, and make you a blessing to many. God is faithful, and He will bless you and bless you real good. Every good and perfect gift comes from God! The greatness that's on the inside of you comes from Him, and it is His will to get the glory out of what He has put on the inside of you! God is so good that He even intends to bless your life by the seeds of greatness that He deposited on the inside of you before you were even born! While you were yet an embryo in your mother's womb, God knew you, and He formed and shaped you to be formed into His image and to do great exploits in the earth realm!

Final story as I come to the end of writing this book. I have been pastoring a church with my husband since 2005. We stepped out on faith and planted a church, starting in our living room. Just before we started the church, I kept hearing God say, "Time is of an essence," and even though no one understood this move we were making, my husband and I obeyed God. Our first members were our children and my oldest sister, Janice. Then her boyfriend Lee joined the church and after that, my husband's brother Rodney joined. Then a few of our neighbors joined with their children and finally, my mother joined us – all while we were still in our living room. We moved from our living room to Elizabeth, and a lot of people from Elizabeth joined the church. They invited family and friends who also joined. The church grew quickly, and we impacted many lives in Elizabeth, New Jersey.

We were led there by prayer and prophecy. I had my youngest daughter Kayla with me as God had instructed me and my husband to go out and find a place for the church to meet outside of our home. I took Kayla and we went and looked at a church in Newark that was for rent. As we were driving away from that church, Kayla spoke from the back seat. She was about seven years old. She said, "Mommy, I don't think God is sending us to Newark."

Surprised to hear her say this, I was even more surprised by my answer. I said, "Really? Where do you think God is sending us?"

She said, "It starts with an E. It's either East Orange, or I think it's Elizabeth."

You could have knocked me over with a very light feather! In my portfolio that was sitting on the passenger's seat in my car, I had two more possible places to look at for our church's new location. One was in East Orange, and the other was in Elizabeth! Also, when I called the East Orange location, it had, all of a sudden, become unavailable, and when we met with the landlord in Elizabeth, he told us that he and his wife had been praying for a church to come and rent that property! They wanted to rent to a church! The planting of our church in our living room and the move to Elizabeth were ordained by God. The people that joined in our living room were mostly unchurched or had not been to church in a while. When God had called us to start the church, He told us that He was sending us for the unchurched!

The assignment changed in Elizabeth. God sent us there to transform His people through the renewing of the mind. The mandate was to usher in a change of mindset amongst the people. We progressed to breaking the spirit of religion and bringing people into a real relationship with God. That's where we are now. It's a Kingdom mandate. Now, as I write this, we are not in a building. We have a social media and conference line ministry and have been doing ministry in this manner since the pandemic struck in March of 2020. It is now March of 2023. We realize that our success as a church and training and equipping center is not tied up in a building. We are still building people and still bringing people into real relationship with God. We don't know what's next, but God does. God told me that when He's finished doing what He's doing in and through us, – when He's finished releasing the greatness that He put inside of us – only He will get the glory.

Keep Dreaming and Keep Digging!

We realize that we just have to keep doing what God has called us to do no matter what disappointments, challenges, setbacks, attacks, or opposition we encounter. During my years of ministry, I've encountered tremendous warfare. Our church went through a "cordial" church split; I have fought through problems in my marriage, things going on with my children, my husband battling cancer, personal health issues, and money problems; I've fought spiritual warfare around my preaching ministry, my books, and my business; I've been ostracized, talked about, rejected, counted out, and cast out. I was pretty much thrown into a figurative pit at one point and felt like my haters were saying, "Now let's see what becomes of this dreamer."

But I kept dreaming! I kept the vision of the greatness that God showed me that was inside of me.

Even though there was warfare all around me, I kept on digging. Much like Isaac and the wells. As he and his men were digging out the wells of his father that the Philistines had filled with dirt, his enemies kept fighting him over the wells, saying that the water was theirs. Isaac didn't go to war against them. He didn't fight them. He just kept moving forward, and He kept on digging until God made room for him and there was no more fighting over what belonged to him.

Just like Isaac, I kept digging. I held my peace and let the Lord fight my battles, and God made room for me. God expanded my territory and ended the strife over what belonged to me and what He had called me to do.

Like Joseph and Isaac, I kept dreaming and I kept digging!

Use your gifts in the prison! Hold your peace and let God fight your battles!

Hold on to your dream and hold on to your shovel! Keep on digging!

Never let go of what God shows you about the greatness inside of you, and never stop doing the work of digging your way out of the dirt and warfare that the enemy will send your way.

The reason I shared our story of church planting is to let you know that you must keep following God's direction even when you can't see where the road is going to end...even when God has shown you success, but it doesn't look like success, or it gets really hard to keep going.

Keep praying. Keep trusting. Keep believing God. He will take you many different ways. You may go through the wilderness, and you may go through some dry places and seemingly barren seasons. As you go, remember that God is taking you somewhere. God will show you when it's time to shift or close shop. He will even sometimes close a door in order to redirect you to walk through another door that He has opened for you. When you go through the shift or the new door, God will use everything that you learned in the old season and in the old place for the new season and the new place.

Sometimes barren seasons and places are used for preparation for where God is taking you! There are no wasted seasons with God! There are no wasted seasons when God is first in your life, and you are following Him.

For I know the plans I have for you, saith the Lord. Plans to prosper you and not to harm you. I have plans to give you hope and a great future. Jeremiah 29:11 paraphrased)

God has a great plan for your life. Your trials and tribulations may have been formed to hurt you, but God is using them for His glory. The haters and dream killers may have tried to kill your ministry or business, stop your purpose, slander your name, or stop you from succeeding, but it won't work! You may have been pushed to the side, pushed to the back, talked about, lied on, lied to, or counted out, but God is still at work in your life. He is using all that you have gone through, will go through, and are going through right now for your good and His glory.

Let me tell you about you the same thing that God told me about me. When God is finished blessing you – when God gets finished doing what He has planned for your life, it's going to blow your mind. When it all comes together, and you walk into your blessed season, when God establishes and promotes you; when you get to the place of great success, and when you are shining forth God's glory as you release the greatness that's inside of you, only God is going to get the glory!

Praise God in the middle of the process!

I dare you to praise God now! Praise God in the middle of the process. Praise God in your wilderness. Praise God in the pit your haters threw you into. Praise God as you climb your way out of the pit. Praise God for every tear you have had to cry. Praise God in the good times and when times look bad. Praise God because when you do, you are truly giving Him the glory! And guess what? God loves praise. He inhabits the praises of His people, and when God shows up, blessings show up. When God shows up, His anointing shows up. When God shows up, the greatness on the inside of you is ignited and activated.

Go ahead and glorify God. Go ahead and praise Him. Go ahead and give God the glory and let your testimony be, God is good all the time and all the time God is good because He put greatness inside of me!" Let your testimony also be, "Everywhere I go, I'm winning. Every time I turn around, I have the victory."

It's Birthing Time

It's time to push out and release the greatness that's kicking inside of you! It's your time to do great things. It's your time to make an impact in the earth realm. It's your time to win and have good success. You got this! Remember to always keep God first, and He will make your name great. He will show forth His power and glory through you as you have victory In every area of your life!

There is power in what you declare out of your mouth. Declare and decree this over your own life:

I was birthed into the earth realm to make an impact. God is ordering my steps to my success! God has ordained my steps to succeed! There is greatness inside of me! It's kicking, and it shall come forth! There is no fear in me. There is no failure in me. There is only victory because God has created me with greatness inside!

Awesome! You have learned the 7 steps to releasing the greatness inside of you. I have a congratulatory gift for you at my website: www.rebeccasimmonsempowers.com

ABOUT THE AUTHOR

Rebecca Simmons is an apostolic and prophetic leader, author of many books, and a certified mentor and coach. She is passionate about her call to speak, preach, prophesy, pastor, write life-changing books, and teach the doctrine of the Kingdom of God, as well as to empower, ignite, and equip other women to walk with power in their Kingdom purpose and victory. She is a powerful speaker who has trained with and received certification from the late Zig Ziglar and the great Les Brown. She has a powerful life story that God is using for His glory. She not only writes and speaks about walking in power and victory, but she has seen what she teaches work in her life. Her goal is to positively impact and change the lives of millions who read her books, listen to her preach or speak, and sit under her mentorship.

Rebecca Simmons attended Rutgers University in Newark and the University of Phoenix in pursuit of a degree in Business. She attended and completed ministry training at Christian Leaders Institute. She received an Honorary Doctorate Degree from Anointed By God Ministries Alliance and Seminary on December 18, 2022.

For the past, 17 years, Dr. Simmons has served as one of the pastors of New Creation Christian Ministries working alongside the Senior

Pastor Anthony Simmons, her husband of almost 27 years. She has four children, four grandchildren, a great grandson and spiritual sons and daughters that she loves and mentors faithfully.

Dr. Rebecca is the Founder of Women Destined for Victory Alliance and Academy where mentors and coaches women to move forward from the pain of the past, to be the best version of themselves, to successfully identify and walk with power and victory in life and in their mandated purpose.

Rebecca Simmons is the author of *Nobody's Business, The Cry of A Woman's Heart, Daddy Love, Don't Die In The Wilderness, Pump Up The Power, Making Marriage And Relationships Work, Man Problems, Moving Forward When Life Lets You Down, You're Better Than That: Real Talk for Ladies Who Want God's Best, God Is A Promise Keeper, Manifesting Kingdom: Unlocking God's Blessings and Abundance In Your Life and Your Book Matters: How To Successfully Write and Publish Your Book.* Her books are available on Amazon.com and wherever books are sold.

Connect with Dr. Rebecca for mentoring: www.womendestinedforvictory.com.

You can find Dr. Rebecca on Facebook @ pastorrebeccasimmons and Instagram @ Pastor_Rebecca_Simmons

ORDER INFORMATION

You can order additional copies of **_Greatness Inside_** by emailing the author directly using the email address below.

Rebecca Simmons

Email Address:

rebeccaempowers@gmail.com

Books are available at the author's website:
www.rebeccasimmonsempowers.com
Amazon.com,
Kindle and Your Local Bookstores (By Request)

Please leave a review for this book on Amazon and let other readers know how much you enjoyed reading it.

Thank you!

www.ingramcontent.com/pod-product-compliance
Lightning Source LLC
Chambersburg PA
CBHW072209090426
42740CB00012B/2448